Pieces of Me

Dreama Cooley

Pieces of Me copyright © 2023 by Dreama Cooley. All rights reserved.

No part of this book may be reproduced, or stored in a retrieval system, or transmitted in any form or by any means, electronic, mechanical, photocopying, recording, or otherwise, without express written permission of the publisher.

ISBN: 9798851948671

Imprint: Independently published

To all my fellow sunflowers

Table of Contents

The Broken Pieces..5

Pieces of Him...45

The Powerful Pieces... 80

The Broken Pieces

May 11th, 1995

On an early Thursday morning....

I pushed my way

through my mother's thick thighs.

"It's a girl!" the doctors shouted.

"I shall call her Dreama,"

my mother whispers.

And then all hell broke loose.

I have never felt safe.

I am always

in constant fear

of losing the most

dearest thing

closest to my heart.

How many times...

will death come

to visit my home?

No one lives there

anymore...

I was always safest

deep inside my mind...

Ever since I was just a child...

Except now...

I cannot find my way out.

-Out my mind

I was never any good
at making friends...
I don't know what
I was so afraid of...

-Loner

The first man

to ever have my heart...

Broke it

into a million little pieces

before any boy ever could...

A million little pieces …

of white rocks,

which he shamelessly smoked

Away...

-My father's keeper

I was a young girl

Who indulged in solitude ...

with a mute tongue

and a heavy heart...

-The Lonely Loner

I always thought proudly
of myself...
As an empath.
Almost like....
it was my superpower.
But...
Imagine how overwhelming
that feels...
To bear the burden
of your own emotions...
On top of *deeply* feeling
everyone else's.
It's quite a daunting task...
One that never ends...
A lifetime of sleepless nights
riddled with other people's feelings...
To think I thought
that this was a gift...
The power to feel others...
even when I didn't want to.
But with each loss
and heartache...
I've realized that
if I must feel things twice
I'd rather feel nothing at all..

I wanted to be you,

maybe even better.

But instead, I am him.

Maybe even worse...

-Mother V Father

"Why do you always have your nose in a book?" My lips stretch into an innocent smile. "Because I am free to go wherever I please."

"And where do you wish to go?" he asks curiously.

"Anywhere but here..."

-Bookworm

You were so high up,

that you could no longer

see us.

And it was much too difficult

to come back down...

I was ripe

with an intense hunger

for love and affection...

Ever since I was

a little girl...

And here I am...

all these years later...

STILL starving...

There are demons
living in places
where they are not
welcome.

-Said my heart

My biggest problem
is not knowing how to be
constant...
With anything or anyone...
Not even myself....

-Self Sabotage

With both their blood

flowing through my veins...

How can I be one

without being the other?

Whatever you were,

He or She...

I'm sure you felt it all

when they tore you out of me...

Your tiny hands and toes...

It must've all hurt so much....

Between my thighs I felt nothing....

And the regret isn't enough...

-Belly of the Beast

I always wondered...
what she searched
for... at the bottom
of that liquor bottle...
Which kissed her lips
to sleep each night.

-The Eldest Daughter

His addiction...

Destroyed us all.

It was as if...

We were addicted

too...

-Child of an Addict

I am always singing...

the same old tune.

And without that tune...

I am nothing.

The tune of a broken heart...

I seem to play it very well.

And without this sad part of me

It's like I have nothing left...

to write about.

Nothing to feel passionate about....

Cause when my heart breaks...

My voice hardens...

My words are strong.

But anything else?

My mind and pen

draws a blank...

And all I'm left with

is sad broken stories

and the same ol sad tune.

-Broken Record

All these men
crowding my head...
Now there's no room
to sleep in my bed...
Cause I'm stuck thinking
about all that they said
What they couldn't do
and everything that I
did...

It's quite exhausting actually.
Constantly going back and
forth with yourself.
One minute I am fine.
The next minute,
I am crippled with pain.
I can feel my heart
trying to justify it...
My mind trying to find
the lesson in it all...
And when this happens...
I can feel my entire body
gasping for air.

-Bipolar

I *always* feel like a soggy rag
that's been hung out to dry...
Twisted and rung
like a wet paper towel...
Constantly being needed...
used...
putting others before me ….
It's drained me...
Leaving literally no time or room
for myself...
Mentally
Emotionally
Physically...
And if I break character...
even just for a second...
Showing any sign of emotion
other than joy
happiness...
Compassion... empathy....
I can literally feel the annoyance
filling the air....
Suddenly I feel like the burden...
A bother to everyone else...
When really, in reality,
its everyone else
who's always bothering me.

-Leave Me Alone

Sometimes my mind gets so clouded...

And it's almost impossible

to hear the good...

So much bad

So many bad thoughts...

They come and go.

But oh, sometimes they stay...

And when these thoughts...

so many bad thoughts …

decides to stay

I can feel my sanity

being stripped away....

And I lose myself...

Then it's nothing but bad...

So many bad thoughts...

-Suicidal Thoughts

I first spread my temple doors

when I was just a child …

Desperate for love,

to feel good.

All around me was shattering...

But I was safe...

inside my precious temple...

Little did I know

that I too was shattering...

from the inside out.

It comes out of nowhere...
I could be home alone....
Or even with a group of friends...
Not doing anything in particular...
When it hits me...
This sudden wave of sadness
Just floods over me...
And for a moment...
I can feel my heart...
I mean *really* feel my heart.
The blood pulsing through it...
the ache behind each pulse.
All the work my heart does
to simply keep me alive...
And it hurts.
The excruciating pain of a broken
heart. It hurts all of a sudden
And not for any specific reason...
But for *every* reason...
Each scar and the story behind it
Old wounds and fresh ones...
I can feel them all
All at once...
all of a sudden,
for no specific reason at all.

All my life...

I have stared into the faces

of doctors...

People who are experts on

what's wrong with me and my

brain... Constantly being told how to

feel. What is right

and

what is wrong.

Ever since I can remember.

Yet I still don't know

"how" to feel...

"Here," they say to me.

"Take these pills, they'll help you

feel better."

Instead, I feel nothing...

Numb...

But don't you see Doctor?

I need to feel *something*,

in order to feel better.

-Pills and potions

I know pain so well...

That it has become a part of me.

I don't know how to be

without it.

It's like....

I feel nothing

and yet

I feel everything

All the same motions

I go through each day,

in hopes that one day

they won't just be "motions"

But instead become life

Moments in which I live,

opposed to simply existing....

Cause that's all I've done lately.

Simply exist...

Waiting for the day

that I live again.

-Dying to live

Most days I roll out of bed...
No energy for brushing my teeth
Or doing my hair...
I'll skip breakfast and lunch
Sometimes dinner as well
Cause I can't seem to find the energy
to simply eat.
I'll drink a bunch of coffee though...
Cause I love the taste of it.
Roll a blunt or two in between cups...
And scroll through social media,
envying the lives
of all the beautiful happy people
across the globe...
Maybe I'll watch Netflix and just chill,
Eat a bag of chips or bunch of candy...
And then finally,
I climb into bed...telling myself
"Tomorrow will be different"
"Tomorrow I will be happy..."
But instead,
I wake up feeling
exactly the same.

-My Depression

For as long as I can remember...

I've always been afraid of the dark....

There was something about the darkness

that seemed to invite

all evil things out to play.

Imagined or real...

They'd crawl from the darkest

corners of my mind...

And watch as I slept.

-The Boogieman

When I was younger

I wanted to be a doctor.

I thought I wanted to save

the whole world...

But I realize now...

All these years later....

I really only wanted to save you.

-I miss you, Mommy

I never did like the girl

Starring back at me...

Her pudgy nose

Bouncy lips,

Wide forehead and sad eyes...

She was always so...

Very

Small...

As if you could crush her

so easily...

And sometimes the world

did just that...

-Insecurities

Sometimes the thought consumes me ...

"What if... I'm not special?"

And in this big world

of so many others...

I really can't change

A goddamn thing worth changing...

No matter how much I may try

and set my dull life ablaze...

It aways burns hopelessly into ashes...

Ashes to ashes...

Dust to dust...

Because maybe I really am nothing more

then a helpless bystander

of my own life.

-Bystander

I always thought achieving

all these "great" accomplishments

would fill whatever was missing

in my life....

Like maybe gaining weight

would make me feel prettier.

Or obtaining exceptional wealth

would feed this intense hunger

I had for life.

But really, in reality...

all these things... these petty little things....

would never change a goddamn thing.

-Lost

Why is it,

That when I look

in the mirror,

the first thing I see,

are all the things

I hate about me?

Doesn't it suck

when you wait a lifetime

for bad news?

You hoped for a happy ending …

Or at least one that made sense....

But in the end,

it's all just sad...

Is everything a lesson?

Or just a bunch of consequences

from sinners and our shitty

choices? Now the realization

is way too heavy to ignore.

And I'm lost in all these feelings....

Is that all we are?

A slave to our emotions?

If so, I'd rather be free

and feel nothing

ever again.

These black clouds?

I know them all too well...

They swallow me whole sometimes...

Trapping me inside of this raging storm

that overwhelms me so much,

until I pour down raining

onto everyone else.

-Raining Pain

Who am I?

I do not know...

Not back then

Maybe not even

now...

What am I searching for

at the bottom of this wine glass?

What am I looking for

at the end of this blunt?

I honestly do not know

So, I keep on searching

looking for a means to an end.

But it never does.

It never ends.

-Coping

Pieces of him

The thought of him

was like coffee and cream.

Bitterly sweet.

Was this really my purpose?
Was I only a pawn in a game
of placing her into your
arms? How can you two
be so happy...
When your love was built
on the hurt and betrayal
of others?

-Bitter

He left me on Thursday...
May 5th, 2016...
Although he had checked out
long before then...
It was moving day for me
and I hugged her goodbye....
My roommate and friend...
never to see her again.
But what I did not know
was that he too had hugged her...
Deciding not to let her go.
Leaving me in a million pieces...
Forever.

-Pieces of you two

I held onto our memories

with shaky, sweaty palms.

It was desperate, I know...

But I thought that maybe...

if I held on tight enough,

new memories would bloom

in place of the old ones.

Little did I know...

You were already making new ones

with everyone else.

You cut me open

and watched me bleed.

Now you're stained

with my blood.

And no matter how

hard you may try,

you'll never be able

to get rid of my blood

staining your hands.

You and me

You and her

Who were you

thinking of...

When you were

with her ….

You and me

or

You and her?

Losing you

was the beginning of

me finding myself.

I find myself doing things

in search of you...

Doing certain things...

only because you used to...

In hopes that maybe

I'd find a way back to you...

But I never really do.

There was a moment between us
when time stood still.
Right before the sun
kissed our skin,
and our eyes were still
blissfully shut.
While I was still tangled in your love,
being smothered by sweet kisses,
breathless "I love You's"
and warm embraces.
It was a time of silence
that rung so loud,
the world around us went mute.
We wanted to stay here forever.
And then the sun comes...
Begging us to get up.

-Mornings with you

Isn't it funny?

You live your entire life without a person, but the moment you fall in love with them, you can never picture being without them.

So how do you go back? How do you go back to living as you were before they came and stole your heart?

After the butterflies have gone away and all that's left is their absence.... How do you go back?

The answer is you don't. You can't go back to who you were before them. Because now you have to move on and decide who you'd like to be after they are long gone.

-Moving on (slowly but surely)

I remember we went to the park

and played tag.

The walk to the park....

all the pushes on the swing...

Suddenly we had no care in the world

We were kids again.

We decided this would be "our spot."

Like the one Ab-Soul rapped about

in "Book of soul."

How we'd meet here

in the end...

Maybe in reincarnation

Maybe just another time in life...

And that no matter what happened...

We'd both make it back

to our spot.

A better you.

A better me.

-Summertime blues

I remember the day...

The first day... you got me all alone in your messy, yet perfect bedroom. "Do you know what lucid dreaming is?" you ask suddenly.

"Yeah," I respond back, trying not to sound smug. "It's when you control what you dream about basically." I take another hit of the perfectly stuffed blunt you rolled and pass it back to you. It was just one of many blunts you had pre rolled and ready for us that day. You were so excited and prepared; it was refreshing to see.

A smile spreads across your face, exposing two perfect

dimples. Without thinking I place my pinky inside and twist gently.

"You're the first girl I ever met who knew,' you say gently. Then, suddenly, a hunger spreads across your face. A strange, almost scary kind of hunger, for me, all of me, every single drop.... But I was not afraid.

Instead, I craved you as well, ready for you to take all of

me, all that I had to offer. You lean in for a kiss, and I hurriedly lean in to meet you, a little too eager to taste those sweet lips and fall hopelessly in love with you.

And that's when I knew... that I'd only ever lucid dream

about you.

#ForMyDreams

It's been quite some time

Since you been away...

In someone else's bed...

giving all my loving' away.

-The room across the hall

I tried to change for you.
Placed my voice in a cage,
and freed my deepest of thoughts.
I opened my soul to the world
Looked for beauty in the darkest of places Turned off all my lights
and faced the darkness head on.
I allowed my soul to sober
and drank from the holy grail
as I lay in the garden of Eden.
Searching for answers
Searching for you
Searching for me....
I bathed in the blood of God
and prayed to be reborn.
I welcomed my most feared emotions
And kissed them with grateful lips
I ran towards the pain
And stood unarmed against my foes
I counted each tear I shed,
tasted my own anguish and despair.
I tried to change for you.
I tried...
My heart was torn into two
My mind raged on with itself...
I tried to change...
Did you?

-Somebody I used to know

I've been losing pieces of myself everywhere...

Hoping that you'd find me somewhere.

I try so hard

not to write about you.

But when the pen

hits the paper...

that's all I want to do.

She was there that entire time.
The night I walked to your mother's...
Hidden there in the basement
Beneath us all.
Right under my nose...
I remember your sister there,
standing between us two...
Your mothers' drunken words
Her slurred truth...
Your secret night together...
Your elderly neighbor from upstairs
trying so hard to console you...
I cried and fought with all my might...
But you were already gone
into her arms...
I begged to stay with you...
But still...
You drove me back home...
Determined to escape me...
To escape us.
It was the shortest yet longest car ride of my life.
And with a weary look in your eyes,
Further away from my heart,
away from me...
You drove me back home leaving me...
forever ...
to continue being with her...

-Our Last Fight

I watched the fires spread

All throughout my head

As I lay in bed

replaying what you said

and all that you did.

I am the girl

You will never mourn for

I am the scar on your heart

You'll never acknowledge.

It's strange...

I know that I am over you. I no longer feel myself waiting on you, hoping you'd call me somehow, praying for you to come back.

I am living without you, as I did before you and as I will do long after you. But there's this small part of me.... a part I know will always be there...

The "what if's"...

They haunt me sometimes... cloud my mind... blur my vision... and it's just so strange. To be completely over someone yet still love them with a small piece of your heart...

-One year later, without you

There's a song I love

And ironically...

it makes me think of you.

Not you and me

But you and her...

And when I'm alone...

Sometimes I cry...

Cause I know I'll spend

the rest of my life,

hearing songs that remind me of you...

That you're thinking of another girl too...

While I'm home alone

still crying over you.

-Pretty little fears

Roll out of bed

A box of reds

Coffee and cigs

Sleep ridden eyes

And messy heads.

-Coffee at your brothers

The way you'd get lost

in your music...

Became my quickest

way to find you.

Your heart.

Your soul.

Your love.

-Music for my soul

I have become those girls

You once confined in me about

The ones you thought you loved...

But realized you

could do without...

-An Ex

I saw it coming

from a mile away...

Yet it still hit me

like a ton of bricks

to the face....

-The End

She was always

such a sad woman.

Her heart had shattered

long ago...

Your patience with her

was thin...

Yet she longed for it....

every single day.

Sometimes she turned

into a monster...

A monster no one was ever

afraid of.

And you all knew that

this monster would be

the death of her in the end.

But I couldn't help to quietly

love her...

Because it was her who brought

you to me...

And if this monster did not exist...

Who would you be?

Your mom shops for dinner
As we giggle and scurry along.
You push the cart into her
Playfully...
She spazzes.
And we laugh uncontrollably.
"Ooouuu baby, smores!"
I smile and give you a kiss.
Who knew grocery
shopping... could be so much
fun?
It was simple.
It was innocent.
It was us.

-Grocery store adventures

Each time I saw

Those perfect dimples...

It was as if

I could simply drown in them....

And I would do so

each time you smiled...

Drowning for you

Again, and again.

-When you smile

I literally dropped to my knees...

begging you to stay.

Little did I know...

You had already planned

your great escape.

One evening,

the cable man came to visit,

and stepped into our smokey gates.

"Do you want a hit?" you asked suddenly,

my favorite smile spreading across your face.

And the chubby, pale skinned man smiled as well,

happily accepting the random offer.

-Random Memories with You

It was so easy for you...

to pretend you were better.

Better than me

Better than everyone....

I imagine

that's what made it

so easy for you.

To only see the bad in others

Even when they so desperately

only saw the good in you...

Even when there was none there.

I am
just another girl
in your arsenal of women.
And only when
you are lonely enough
to soothe your raging pain...
Is when you suddenly
get a taste for me.
Or maybe it's an old song
that now pertains to us so well
that reminds you of something
so long gone...
But either way...
I am such a fool for you
that I will be used however
you need me to be.
And maybe... just maybe...
you are already very quite aware
of this blind devotion I have for you.
This hunger, that only you can feed.
Maybe that's why you think of me...
I want to stand out
in the crowd standing in front of you.
I want to be seen by you, to be special...
But I am in fact, just one of many.
One of the many girls
in love with you....

-My favorite person to write about

There's a rainbow
in your bathroom...
But there isn't any pot of gold
waiting at the end of it...
Just demons and all your
disappointments....
The last six years
stretched between us....
are filled with moments
that I don't know....
Who is this guy
staring back at me?
A ghost from my past,
belonging to a different part of me.
We were so young, so wild and free.
But now father time has gotten between
you and me.
I feel like I'm dreaming,
a lucid dream...
But all dreams
must come to an end.
And wasn't that what were
in the end?
Just another tragic ending
to such a beautiful beginning....

-All this time later....

I was obsessed with this idea of you

The idea that you were "The One."

You see really,

what was so special about you...

was my desire to not let you go...

This hunger I had for the past....

I'm realizing now that

I never gave myself credit.

It was always about you

and why you were so special.

As if I lacked superpowers on my own...

But see, I too am magical.

And together...

that made us special.

Not just you.

But me and you.

I am still special all on my own.

And with that realization...

I've suddenly and finally

let you go.

-Closure

The Powerful Pieces

One night....

My mind and body woke up screaming.

And I did not know what was wrong...

"What do you need me to do?" I pleaded.

"Close our temple doors!" they cried out.

"We have no room for anyone else."

It takes courage

to place your heart

in the hands of others.

But it takes much more

to place your heart

in the hands of yourself.

-Self Love

Although different blood
flowed through our veins
She loved me as if
our blood was the same.
My mother to me
in all the right ways...
When my world went dark
she prayed for brighter days...
Despite the mindless acts
and rebellions I threw
I never lost sight
of the guidance from you.
You taught me to love
and how to truly trust.
And I just want to say "thank you"
In case I haven't said it enough.

-Mama Mary

One thing I have learned
is that with pain
beauty always follows.
And if you're not careful
you'll let the pain take it all
away.

-Collateral Beauty

I met her in a dream.
Her name was Ellie.
Her face was strange,
as a trunk and tusks
sprouted from it....
Yet she died a human
and was reborn
as this beautiful creature.
She told me all
without saying one word...
Her black eyes held wisdom
beyond my years.
She was huge compared to me...
But moved with such grace.
I wondered what this moment meant...
The one I shared with the phantom elephant.
And as if she read my thoughts,
the answer came shortly after.
Suddenly I felt strong.
The pain of my reality became my lesson.
As her compassion and femineity overwhelmed
me, my most painful moments became wisdom.
I was not weak. I was not lonely.
I was powerful like Ellie.
I too was graceful.
And as Ellie slowly faded from my dreams
and became a new beautiful memory,
I silently thanked her for her wisdom,
And slowly awoke from my deep slumber.

-Ellie l'elefante

I've let too many men

take refuge inside my mind

long after they've decided to leave...

But what I had not realized...

is that with doing such a foolish thing

I have left no room for myself.

-Refugees of my heart

I've spent too much time

dying in the past...

When I could be living

here in the present.

-Stuck

After ignoring them
for so long...
My mind, body and soul
has finally confronted me
and walked us all back home,
where we belong.

-Homebody

I've let the opinions of others

define me for so long

that I almost drowned in it.

Yet here I am, still breathing,

trying to find my way back to shore.

-Just keep swimming

I had a dream that it was
the first day of high school
And all of my friends
were waiting excitedly for me
outside of homeroom...
And suddenly...
I miss my childhood
I miss how we all knew
every minor and major detail
of each other's lives.
The simplicity of friendship
without having to fit each other
into our busy adult lives...
Now filled with careers, relationships
and children of our own.
The fun filled
drunken nights,
late night sleepovers...
Grabbing a bite after school...
Spilling our guts over some burgers and
fries... I miss it
My youth...
Belonging to a group of people
bigger than just me.
My family away from family...
I miss it all
so very much.

Sometimes....

I get so lost

in who I want to be, that

I completely forget how far

I've come to be who I am

right now.

-Progress

These men

are simply visitors

here in our goddess's temple.

And when it's time to go

We must escort them back to

wherever the hell they came from

and lock all our doors.

-Visiting hours are over

I've wasted too many of my words

telling the same story of the past...

-Letting Go

I thought it was solitude

that my soul ached for...

I thought I was lonely

due to keeping the wrong company...

But suddenly I realized...

I was so alone because

I was the only one

still living in the past....

I now take pride

in my solitude,

not shame or pity.

Because how brave is it

to face everything all on your own?

I have left my joy in the past
for far too long...
But now, I am strong enough
to go and take it back.

And although their apologies

never even came,

I forgave them both,

nonetheless.

-The Bigger Person

These past seven years....

has taught me so much

I couldn't even begin

to write it all down,

even if I wanted to.

But through the chaos

and necessary heart aches,

I find myself broken and shattered.

As usual.

But stronger than ever before.

His tiny smile

And endless "I love Yous",

Filled my lungs with life

on the days I was too weak

to fill them myself.

-Motherhood

I offered you my temple

a safe haven for your growth.

To flourish and blossom

into the precious little flower planted

in my soul.

To stay there forever...

long after we are gone...

It was there you grew.

And stretched.

Kicked and yawned.

Smiled and hiccupped,

until you sprouted from within me.

To bloom here in the world, finally.

And with a stitch and faint cry,

you changed my life

and *became* it, all at once.

-February 11th, 2018, 2:13 pm

You call my name

a million times a day.

And you can bet I'll be there

every time that you do.

No matter the age

No matter the problem

Good news or Bad news...

I promise too always be there for you.

-unconditional love

Only after the birth

of my first born...

Would I realize that

I am a goddess.

My body is a holy temple.

Capable of creating life within life.

-The circle of life

Twin flames were born

And then we met...

Higher than the clouds

So far away we get...

Though our blood isn't the same

our souls are just alike.

Two stars under the moon

Best friends for life.

-Earl Smith

Dedicated to my best friend

We as women

must stick together.

Cause this is a man's world.

And when the world comes

to take our power and freedom,

it is only us together

who can take it back.

-Feminist

The amount of pressure

society places on the backs of women

would shatter a thousand nations of

men but could never shatter them.

I was the little girl
who wore glasses
and was much too timid to speak.
I liked anime and video games
and books filled with so much love
that it was impossible to feel alone.
My skin hugged my bones
and my breast never sprouted very
far. I wasn't very popular
or had lots of friends.
I was always picked last,
if I was even picked at all.
I sat alone in class,
got lost in the crowd...
And for a long time, I felt odd...
Like I didn't belong anywhere
Just stumbling through life...
Always so out of step.
The one puzzle piece that didn't fit.
But I finally realized
all these years later....
That I'd rather be odd and strange
then to be like everyone else
who was exactly the same.

-Weirdo

Wild curly mane

Sprouting from her dome

The roots of Africa

Her birth home...

Her skin can warm you

Watch her melanin drip

The curve of her hips

The fullness of her lips

Through the world's eyes

She'll never be free...

But she is you

Don't you see?

They don't think of Africa

When they think of beauty

Still proud to be

Africa is me

She is you

She is me.

-African American

Flowers are the perfect

metaphor of life.

When we are young,

We are bright and colorful

Beautiful and delicate...

And then we wither

as we get older.

Become dull and wrinkly

Limp and weak

Until we wilt and fall

Back to the earth

Only to be reborn more beautiful

than before.

-Mother Earth and all of her

children

One night I had a dream that I woke up in heaven
and had a cup of coffee with God.
He drank his as is.
No cream, no sugar. Just black.
He smiled the kind of smile
that said he was proud of you.
That he understood.
I felt like a small child in his presence.
No worries, no fears. I was safe.
Truly content in the simplicity of life.
To just be alive and be me.
It truly was a grand thing.
He passes my cup, two creams, two sugars.
Just the way I like it.
It tastes like every goal and dream I hoped to
accomplish. Would accomplish...
It was the best cup of coffee
I ever had. So, I cried.
Happily.
Tears of gratitude, tears of joy.
And he wipes them away so swift and gracefully,
they hardly get the chance to kiss my cheeks.
Suddenly I laugh, quietly, happily.
Because how powerful are we?!
That we can feel emotions so strong
it brings the ocean to our eyes?
God laughs too. It's heartfelt.
The sound fills the air and soothes my soul.
He takes my hand, and we walk off.
I am safe. Secure.
It was as if I was never asleep at all.

-Coffee in Heaven

I am
absolute chaos...
A beautiful fire
raging within...

My soul longed

to sing.

But my voice

had yet to blossom.

-This Voice Inside of Me

The bitterness will eventually turn sweet.

And stick to your soul

like honey.

-Healing

"If I told you I was writing a book about other people's view on me, what would you say?"

The question was random, and he took a second to respond.

"You want me to tell you how I feel about you?"

"Yeah, basically" I say shrugging. He smiles.

"You'll have to give me a second, that's a loaded question." He sits quietly for a moment, tugging at his long locs before finally responding. My hands feel clammy suddenly.

"I think you're anti-social, but you want to get out and meet new people. You just never seem to have the energy. You're caring but you can also be very selfish at times. You're beautiful, like really beautiful. But most times you just can't see it. You're still trying to find yourself, trying to balance the mom title and your own personal life. You're silly but only with people you're comfortable with. You can be a very cranky woman sometimes, but you hate that you get that way. You have such a beautiful, contagious smile. Chef Dreams. Also, you're the queen of self-sabotage. You want to be happy, but you don't know what truly brings you happiness... and your smile could light up the darkest of rooms."

"Wow," I say quietly, my eyes filling with tears. "She sounds pretty cool."

You look at me and smile. "Yeah, she does."

-The perfect Point of View

How beautiful is she?

The human heart.

Who dies a thousand deaths

without ever truly dying.

-Heartache

With just two more years
left of my twenties....
I realize my youth...
has come to a sudden end,
and been replaced with wisdom.
The kind of wisdom that only comes after tough lessons and years of grace.

If I'm being honest...
I like making men
fall hopelessly in love with me...
Giving them a taste of
something they'll crave
for the rest of their life.
Making them laugh
with my eyes...
Hypnotizing them
with my smile...
It's like...
I am in control of them...
Like I could rob them
for everything they own...
With no weapons needed...
And they'd happily hand
everything over to me...
Just as long as they
can get a taste of my sweet
unforgettable lovin'
But didn't their doctors warn them?
Someone as sweet as me
Isn't EVER good for their health.

There are some people who are so frightened by the idea of being alone (myself once included) that they are willing to give any part of themselves to anyone capable of making them feel "whole." And how sad is that?

That it's easier to depend on the company of others to make you feel complete than it is to be in your own presence. When did that become okay? Exposing your heart again and again. Despite its previous battles, the wars lost.

Why is it easy to place our hearts in the hands of others but not our own? Who taught us that? Who taught us that the best love comes from someone else? Who told us that self-love wasn't enough, if not better?

I do not know where this fear of solitude came from. I do not understand this rapid hunger to be loved. It's everywhere, for everyone. But ourselves.

-My Generation of Love

There are moments in life which are filled with so much pain, you'd rather die than bear through it. As if there was no such thing as an end, as if this excruciating pain would only worsen with time.

We've all been there before. Hurt. Crippled. Shattered. But

despite how unbearable the pain may have been, you now have wings strong enough to carry you to the sky. You'll be able to look back on those moments you swore you wouldn't get through and smile.

You're going to smile so big, until all the muscles in your face begin to cramp, until your pretty wings carry you higher and higher. So high that it would take all the angels above the clouds to carry you back down.

-Pretty Wings

Do not hide from me

when my fire starts

and you're afraid of the flames.

Do not run from me

when my words harden

and you don't know what to

say. Stand your ground instead.

Because this is just one

of many battles in a war

I fight within

every single day.

And I don't need any weak men

defending my sanity and peace

as we fight these demons

living here with me.

So, stand tall my soldier,

Against all my raging emotions.

Don't run.

Don't hide.

But stand with me,

Side by side.

"Why is it so hard for you to let go of others?" he asked suddenly.

The smell of coffee and cigarettes clung to my tongue as I spoke.

"Because I know how it feels when others gave up on

me."

I escaped

Before it was much too late

Or I am afraid I too,

would have suffered

the same fate.

-My sister's keeper

We were best friends

long before

we were brother and sister.

You taught me how love

can hurt a boy who's not ready

and break a girl who's ready too

soon. You get an idea, and it sticks to

you like we stuck together as kids.

Life would try to tear us apart

and I'd put love before you

again, and again.

Yet you never judged

when I came back home,

tail tucked and smelling of defeat.

And finally, I realized

all these years later

when these boys leave my heart

empty and cold

there is always a spot in yours

warmer than all those boys

combined.

-Little "Big" Brother

I want to be...

fed from the soul...

To be taken care of

Deeper than physical means

Mentally

Spiritually

Selflessly

To be fed with love

And empathy

Kindness and light

Understanding and

commitment Spontaneously

Romantically

Sexually....

My soul is aching for a love

I fear I'll never get a taste of.

Greet me with love...

The kind of love

that warms me

the moment I walk

through the door.

The kind that melts

away my anger

when my heart feels

too heavy.

Greet me with empathy

And passion

Kindness

And understanding.

So, I can greet you

The very same way

I'd like you to greet me.

-Meet me halfway

I don't want

to have you

for financial stability.

All though help

with the bills

would be nice.

What I need from you

I cannot be able to do...

on my own...

To be nurtured...

Mentally...

Spiritually...

Sexually...

Emotionally...

This is what I need...

What I want...

All that I lack...

You must have...

Because if not...

What good would you be

To me then???

Sometimes sadness comes to visit

And she won't knock,

She'll come suddenly,

loud and consuming

sometimes quietly and unnoticing...

But still,

let her in.

Sit with her and talk

about all the places it hurts...

Kiss her wounds

with patient, gentle lips

and wipe her tears away.

Wrap her in your arms

and tell her

"it'll be okay soon."

She'll sit in silence for a while

It may even feel like a lifetime

But just as you promised

It'll all be okay, and she'll be gone

long before you know it.

-Until next time old friend

The older I get

The more of you

I see in me...

In my smile...

In my son...

As time passes by...

The closer I get

To you....

Despite the fact

You're no longer here.

-Rest peacefully, Mommy

You always called for nothing at all. Most of the time, it was just to hear my voice. I never had to do much to earn your pride. Simply being your daughter brought you joy. We were all the pride of your life. No one worked harder than you "OT". And when the silence stretched between us and the years of regret clung to your lips, I painfully wished that I was kinder to you. I wish I told you that I understand your pain, how losing mommy tore you apart. You simply could not function without your heartbeat... And that's who mommy was to you. Your heart outside your body... And when she died, a piece of you died as well. You'd spend the rest of your life trying to find that missing piece, trying to make up for the mistakes you made as a father and as a husband. But daddy, little did you know, you had already paid your debt, you were already forgiven. You were so much more than the mistakes you made... You were a ray of sunshine in the darkest of rooms... Such a true reliable worker that you literally spent your last breath on the job... not in the warmth of your bed, surrounded by family, or a noisy, bright hospital room. But at work, on the job, helping others... And in the absence of your love and your pointless phone calls, I realize now those pointless phone calls had a point all along. It was the only way you knew how to show you loved me, and I hope you knew how much I loved you too.

-Rest peacefully Dad

You smell like

Every hope and dream

I ever wished to come true...

Can I have a taste of you?

Love and Sadness...
are like the oldest of friends...
I like to think those are
some of our most primal
feelings...
It's something so peculiar about
the two...
You can't have one
without the other...
At some point, in Love,
there will be Sadness.
And at some point, in Sadness,
there will be Love...
Almost like they happily co-exist
with each other
When we are Sad,
we need Love...
And with Love there will
no doubt be Sadness...
Rather from death or heartache
Sadness will come.
And when she does
who do you think saves her?
Love does.

I've spent my entire life
living uncomfortable
in my own skin.
Yet I still somehow
brought men to their knees
without even trying to.
But...
Imagine the nations of men
I'd bring to my feet
if I awakened this goddess
slumbering deep within me?

Life sat me down

And forced me to write

About all the things

I didn't even know

I needed to write

about.

I want to be free...
Free of everyone's expectations...
Even my own...
I want to fly across the world
With my baby boy by my side
Exploring mother earth and all
She has to offer her flower children...
To return within
deep inside my temple....
Where I become closer with self
No longer dependent on
the company of others
or their temporary love...
To write Love a novel
of all the times she's made me
cry tears of joy
and tears of pure anguish...
To sing a song to Death
about all the people I miss
that are now living with him.
To meet God on my own terms
And become one with prayer and
faith. I want to become anew...
to be born again under a golden sun...
My old petals wilting away...
Returning to mother earth
where we all belong.
Only to bloom yet again
more beautiful than before.

-The rebirth

I am the town surrounding
the bright city.
A place no one
ever thinks to visit...
but falls hopelessly in love with
the moment they finally do.
The stars shine brighter here
Cause the city only dims
them... There's no loud noise
or distractions....
Just breathe taking beauty...
The air feels lighter...
smells peaceful...
Suddenly the silence
is all you ever wanted....
Because now,
you can hear your thoughts
more clearly than ever before.
Love, Pain, Joy....
You feel them all, suddenly...
But you aren't afraid...
Because you left your fears
back in the city....
And once you leave,
you'll never want
to come back.

-What it's like loving me

These scars are proof

that I am alive.

A reminder of how strong

I really am.

This is my journey of life...

How I have survived

heartache and death

Sorrow and misery

Love and happiness

Twenty-eight years

of my life bled onto

a blank canvas...

The window to my soul

now sits in your hand...

The sad pieces,

happy pieces,

and the powerful ones.

We did it. We both made it to the end of this journey. Together. And now that you have a window to my soul, I'd like to thank you for being so kind and listening to me. Life is hard as it is on its own without reading about other people's lives. I wish I could hug you. Cover you in my deepest appreciation for sitting through my pain, struggle and joy with me. To kiss your cheeks with great gratitude. I hope I have given you some sense of relief in knowing that we all go through the same emotions, just different experiences. May the sun forever shine down on you and may you always stay rooted and connected to our mother earth. Until next time, my flower brothers and sisters.

-love letter to my readers

About the Author

Born in Buffalo, New York, writing has always been Dreama's love language. Ever since she can remember, writing has soothed her more than anything else in the world. Unable to get the idea of her book out of her mind; at age twenty-eight, she finally self-published "Pieces of Me." She enjoys time in the sun, decorating blank canvases with paint and writing about whatever plagues her mind and soul.

"Let my words heal you in all of the places you don't speak of..."

Made in United States
North Haven, CT
25 October 2023